Great Beaded Gifts

Great Beaded Gifts

Linda Gettings

Sterling Publishing Co. Inc. New York
A Sterling/Chapelle Book

Chapelle, Ltd.:
Jo Packham, Sara Toliver, Cindy Stoeckl, Matt DeMaio

Book Design: Dan Emerson, Pinnacle Marketing
Photographer: Ryne Hazen

If you have any questions or comments, please contact:
Chapelle, Ltd., Inc., P.O. Box 9252, Ogden, UT 84409
(801) 621-2777 • (801) 621-2788 Fax
e-mail: chapelle@chapelleltd.com
Web site: www.chapelleltd.com

Space would not permit the inclusion of every decorative item photographed for this book, nor could all of the designers be identified. Many of these items are available by contacting:
Ruby & Begonia, 204 25th Street, Ogden, UT 84401
(801) 334-7829 • (888) 888-7829 Toll-free
e-mail: ruby@rubyandbegonia.com
Web site: www.rubyandbegonia.com

Library of Congress Cataloging-in-Publication Data

Gettings, Linda.
 Great beaded gifts / Linda Gettings.
     p. cm.
 Includes index.
 ISBN 1-4027-1394-0
 1. Beadwork. I. Title.

TT860.G46 2005
745.58'2--dc22
                                                        2004026685
10 9 8 7 6 5 4 3 2 1
Published in paperback in 2007 by Sterling Publishing Co., Inc.
387 Park Avenue South, New York, NY 10016
©2005 by Linda Gettings
Distributed in Canada by Sterling Publishing
c/o Canadian Manda Group, 165 Dufferin Street
Toronto, Ontario, Canada M6K 3H6
Distributed in the United Kingdom by GMC Distribution Services,
Castle Place, 166 High Street, Lewes, East Sussex, England BN7 1XU
Distributed in Australia by Capricorn Link (Australia) Pty. Ltd.
P. O. Box 704, Windsor, NSW 2756, Australia

Printed and Bound in China
All Rights Reserved

Sterling ISBN-13: 978-1-4027-1394-1 Hardcover
         ISBN-10: 1-4027-1394-0
         ISBN-13: 978-1-4027-3385-7 Paperback
         ISBN-10: 1-4027-3385-2

For information about custom editions, special sales, premium and corporate pur-
chases, please contact Sterling Special Sales Department at 800-805-5489 or
specialsales@sterlingpub.com

Preface

I have been interacting with beaders, both fledglings and experienced, by teaching classes and talking to the many customers that come into the bead shop. If I have learned anything, it is that beginning beaders are anxious to learn new techniques and experienced beaders are always looking for something new and different. In *Great Beaded Gifts*, beaders of all levels will find a project of interest.

There is a wonderful diverse mixture of jewelry, gifts, and home decorating projects that is sure to be great fun making and giving as gifts to friends and family.

So, for all you beaders, my hope is that you'll have as much fun making these gifts as your friends have receiving them.

Linda G

Table of Contents

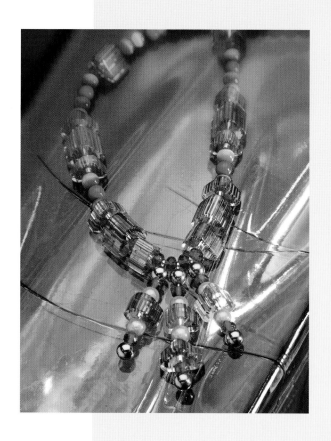

General Instructions

Beading Notions

Before we begin, here is some basic information for making your beading experience easier and more fun. To get started, there are some basic beading notions and tools that you will need for most projects. These consist of:

Beading Needles & Needle Threader

I like to have these in sizes 10 and 12. They have a very small eye and you may need to use a needle threader as the needle is stiff and the thread is a bit wobbly. Try "needling the thread" instead of threading the needle.

Beading Thread

Most beading teachers alternate the use of double and single thread, depending on the project. A design that takes the thread through a bead two or three times will work better with a single thread. If the design only takes the thread through beads once, doubling will be a more secure way of putting a piece together.

It is best to use as much thread as you are comfortable with. I suggest at least 3'; the less you have to add later the better. It might take a little getting use to, but using 6' of thread at a time is ideal.

Ruler or Tape Measure

A 60" vinyl-coated tape measure works best.

Scissors

I prefer to use small sharp scissors. They are easier to handle and use.

Thread Conditioner

It is always a good idea to condition the thread with either beeswax or thread conditioner. Conditioning helps to cut down on tangles and gives the thread more strength.

Work Surface

I use a bead tray with a leather or suede liner. The tray liner will keep the small beads from rolling around and the tray will allow you to move about with the project should you care to go out on the porch, to the pool or beach, on an airplane, or anywhere you need a portable surface.

Basic Techniques

Adding New Thread

There are only two ways to do this. 1. Bury the old thread by taking the needle and thread in and out of a number of side-by-side beads in the piece until the thread is secure, then snip off the excess. Add new thread in the same way, exiting where the old thread left over, and continue beading. 2. Tying on a new thread. This requires you to tie on the new thread to the old thread, using a secure knot. I prefer the square knot. *Note: You can add a small dab of glue for additional security.*

Whichever knot you choose, be certain it is very secure and will not untie before continuing the project. In some cases, you may need to bury the knot before continuing. Weave around the piece as necessary to hide the old and get back to the place where you stopped.

Crimping

String a crimp bead and one end of the closure. You can string on an 11/0 seed bead between the crimp and the closure if desired.

Go back through the seed bead and crimp, going an additional ½" for extra security. Squeeze the crimp bead with either flat-nosed pliers or the crimping tool. *Note: If using a crimping tool, place the crimp in the back dip and squeeze, move the crimp up to the front dip and turn one-fourth turn, then crimp again. This will fold the crimp onto itself and add extra security as well as be more attractive.*

Fixing a Mistake

There are only two ways. 1. Take out the beads all the way back to the mistake. 2. Learn to live with it.

Picot Edging

Quite a few of the projects found herein will include a picot edge. To create a picot, take the needle and thread out of the piece in the desired spot, pick up three beads, and take the needle back through the same place that you exited. This will cause the three beads to form a triangle or picot edge.

Putting It All Together

This can be done many ways. Creating a matching jewelry set—necklace, bracelet, and earrings; or if you enjoy knitting, a scarf, scarf pin, and hatband are putting it all together. This technique can be done with any of the projects in this book if the right beads are used.

Stopper Bead

A stopper bead is a small bead that has 3 or 4 slipknots around it to keep it in place. This bead will be left in place and buried in the design.

Waste Bead

A bead that is added at the beginning but removed later. Tie two slipknots around a waste bead to secure it. Remove the waste bead anytime after 4–5 rows.

A design using a stitch such as flat peyote may even have waste rows that will be removed later.

Bead Shopping

Finding the perfect beads is not always easy. I suggest checking with your
local bead shop first. If the store does not have what you're looking for, they
may be willing to suggest another location or order them. If you do not
have a local bead store, you may find some of the materials and beads you
need at your local craft store. If you don't have either, or your local craft
store does not carry what you are looking for, get yourself a copy of one of
those great beading magazines, check out a few mail-order catalogs, or
search the Internet.

*Easy
Beaded
Jewelry*

Black & Gold Necklace

This simple-to-create necklace is a great quick gift for a beginning or experienced beader.

MATERIALS

- BEADS:

    Assorted

- Beading Notions on page 8
- Crimping tool or flat-nosed pliers
- Crimps (2)
- Flexible beading wire
- Toggle clasp or lobster claw clasp and jump ring
- Wire cutters

INSTRUCTIONS

1. Cut wire to desired length plus 1".
2. Attach first clasp half to one end, using crimp. See Crimping on page 9.
3. String beads onto wire as shown above or as desired.
4. Attach second clasp half, using crimp.

Note: To make a matching bracelet, follow the instructions above, using the correct length of wire.

Variation: This tan set mixes semiprecious and metal beads. The necklace was made following the instructions for Black & Gold Necklace on page 14 and the bracelet was made using stretch cord. See Red and Black Stretch Cord Bracelet on page 16.

Red & Black Stretch Cord Bracelet

This is by far the quickest way to make a bracelet. Stretch bracelets are quite popular and can be made in any pattern.

MATERIALS

- BEADS:

    Assorted

- 1mm–wide stretch cord

- E–6000 adhesive

INSTRUCTIONS

1. Cut stretch cord to desired size.

Note: Leave at least one finger width between the bracelet and your wrist. This will make the bracelet look and feel better once beads are added. I leave an additional 1½" to tie the knot.

2. String beads as shown above or as desired.

3. Tie loose ends in a knot.

4. Cover knot completely with glue.

5. Trim excess cord down to knot.

Note: The glue will hold the knot closed and the beads should cover the knot completely.

Variations: Charms can be added intermittently, in a pattern, or singly when adding beads to stretch cord as in the bracelets at top left and bottom of photo. To add hanging beads to a bracelet, like the one shown at top right, use the Bend-cut-curl technique on page 120, attaching the head pins onto stretch cord instead of earring wires.

Turquoise & Brown Necklace

Turquoise and brown are not two colors I usually think of together; so when I found this great focal bead, I knew I had to do this necklace.

MATERIALS

- BEADS:

    Assorted

    Focal

    Seed (for anchor)

- Beading Notions on page 8
- Crimping tool or flat-nosed pliers
- Crimps (2)
- Flexible beading wire
- Lobster claw clasp and jump ring

INSTRUCTIONS

1. Attach first clasp half and one crimp to one side of wire, using crimping tool.

2. String beads as desired to approximately halfway point.

3. Thread wire's loose end through focal bead and one smaller bead that will act as an anchor. Bring wire through anchor bead, focal bead, and two previous beads before focal bead.

4. Add remaining beads and second clasp half, then crimp.

5. To add fringe, thread a needle with 1' of thread.

6. Take thread through anchor bead so that half hangs on each side.

7. Pick up fringe beads as desired, running thread back up through all fringe beads and knot thread at top.

8. Cut off excess thread.

Note: The bracelet with the square toggle closure was made following the instructions for the Black & Gold Necklace on page 14, using the correct size of wire. The second bracelet was made following the instructions for Red & Black Stretch Cord Bracelet on page 16. The earrings in this photograph were made following instructions for the Bend-cut-curl Technique on page 120.

TIP:
I have found that the tubular-shaped crimps hold better than the small round crimps.

Here's an easy way to make a complete jewelry set. Coordinating necklace, bracelets, and earrings make great gifts for anyone who likes to wear jewelry. Note: The colors used are picked up from the focal bead, as I always try to do when creating a piece.

Necklace
MATERIALS

- BEADS:
    3mm round
    11/0 seed
    Coordinating
    Faceted rondelle
    Focal
    Square faceted
- Beading Notions on page 8
- Flexible beading wire
- Wire cutters

INSTRUCTIONS

1. Follow instructions for Black & Gold Necklace on page 14, adding fringe as follows:

    a. Add focal bead by stringing wire from top to bottom. At bottom of focal bead, pick up (3) 11/0 seed, (1) faceted rondelle, (3) 11/0 seed, (1) 3mm round, (3) square faceted, (1) 3mm round, and (1) 11/0 seed beads.

    b. Thread wire back through all beads and continue stringing beads to complete necklace.

Note: The matching Bracelet was made following the instructions for the Red & Black Stretch Cord Bracelet on page 16. The earrings are made using the Bend-cut-curl Technique on page 120. The head pins were attached onto an earring disk. Follow instructions for the Black & Gold Necklace on page 14, using the correct sized wire to make the black and green bracelet shown in photo at right.

TIP:
I use stretch cord when I think I might want to cut a piece apart later and do something more elaborate.

This easy technique allows you to create matching earrings for any necklace or bracelet. This set mixes semiprecious, glass, and metal beads, and is what I like to call "denim friendly."

Earrings

MATERIALS

- BEADS:

    Assorted

- Beading Notions on page 8
- Earring wires (2)
- Head pins (2)
- Round-nosed pliers
- Wire cutters

INSTRUCTIONS

1. String beads onto head pins as shown in photograph above.

2. Attach beaded head pins to earring wires, using the Bend–cut–curl Technique on page 120.

Note: To make the necklace, follow the instructions for the Black & Gold Necklace on page 14, adding a seed bead between the crimp and clasp.

If you come across a holeless bead that you know will be just perfect for a necklace for that certain someone, don't panic. Simply follow these instructions to add a button back and then string as usual.

MATERIALS

- BEADS:

    Assorted

    Holeless flat-backed focal

- Beading Notions on page 8
- Button back
- Crimping tool or flat-nosed pliers
- Crimps (2)
- E-6000 adhesive
- Toggle clasp

INSTRUCTIONS

1. Center and adhere button back onto the flat back of holeless bead. Let dry at least three hours or overnight.

2. Follow instructions for Black & Gold Necklace on page 14, adding focal bead at halfway point.

Pearl & Crystal Jewelry Set

I never appreciated a strand of pearls. Then, two years ago I made someone a Mother's bracelet using pearls, spacer beads, and crystals representing birthstones. I loved it so much that I started doing a few more things with pearls.

Necklace
MATERIALS

- BEADS:

    5.5mm pearl (45)

    6mm faceted lavender crystal (14)

    Small flat spacer (62)

- Beading Notions on page 8
- Crimping tool or flat-nosed pliers
- Crimps (2)
- Flexible beading wire
- Toggle clasp
- Wire cutters

INSTRUCTIONS

1. Cut wire to desired size.

2. Follow instructions for the Black & Gold Necklace on page 14, stringing beads as shown in photo at right or as desired.

Note: For a longer necklace, add more crystals and pearls.

Bracelet
MATERIALS

- BEADS:

    5.5mm pearl (17)

    6mm faceted lavender crystal (17)

    Small flat spacer (72)

- 5mm open jump rings (2)
- Beading Notions on page 8
- Crimping tool or flat-nosed pliers
- Crimps (2)
- Double-bar ends (2)
- Flexible beading wire
- Toggle clasps

INSTRUCTIONS

1. Cut two pieces of same-sized wire to desired size.

2. Attach one end of each wire to double bar, using crimp.

3. Pick up beads as shown in photo at right or as desired.

Note: I alternate each strand so that when worn, a pearl and a crystal sit next to each other.

4. Attach second ends onto double bar, using crimp, then add toggle clasp to each end.

Earrings
MATERIALS

- BEADS:

    5.5mm pearl (12)

    6mm faceted lavender crystal (2)

    Small flat spacer (16)

- Beading Notions on page 8
- Ear wires (2)
- Head pins (6)
- Round-nosed pliers
- Triple-bar ends (2)

INSTRUCTIONS

1. Using the Bend-cut-curl Technique on page 120, string pearls, spacers, and crystals.

2. Attach head pins onto triple-bar ends.

3. Attach ear wires onto triple-bar single-loop ends.

How many pairs of glasses do you think a person misplaces in their lifetime? Why? They put them down while they are shopping, or set them in the grass while watching a soccer game. No matter where glasses are placed, sometimes you have to wonder if they will ever turn up again. I think any woman would love to get this glass-saving gift!

MATERIALS

- BEADS:

    Assorted

- Crimping tool or flat-nosed pliers

- Crimps (2)

- Flexible beading wire
  (30"–34" long)

- Eyeglass vinyl end grips (2) or
  expandable circular grip (1)

- Wire cutters

INSTRUCTIONS

1. Make a bead "soup" by mixing different-sized beads in a pleasing color palette.

Note: You can use your leftover beads and mix them together or buy new beads and mix them together in a bowl. For the black/brown/gray chain, I used jasper and glass beads in an alternating pattern.

2. Attach one end onto expandable circular grip, using crimp.

3. String beads as desired, leaving 2" at wire's end.

Note: The fastest way to string the beads onto the beading wire is to make a pile of beads and run the tip of the wire through the pile a couple of times.

4. Attach remaining end onto expandable circular grip, using crimp.

Note: Repeat Steps 1–4 above to create the copper-turquoise chain, except the ends will be crimped onto eyeglass vinyl grip ends. The black/brown/gray eyeglass holder would make a great gift for a more conservative recipient. Cut the desired size wire in half and attach one end of each onto a circular grip. Bead each half identically and attach the free ends onto the ring.

TIP:

If you love to wear sunglasses and are always losing them (sometimes even on the top of your head), make a few holders in colors to match and hang them around your neck!

Changeable Bead Necklace

Changeable bead bars are a popular addition to any beaded necklace. Give this necklace as a gift to anyone who likes to change the look of their jewelry on a regular basis. There are endless possibilities.

MATERIALS

- BEADS:

    3.5mm round (16–20)

    4mm faceted spacer (25–30)

    6mm round (60)

    Assorted art glass (18–20)
- Beading Notions on page 8
- Cellophane tape
- Changeable bead bars (3)
- Closed or spring ring and jump ring
- Crimping tool or flat-nosed pliers
- Crimps (2)
- Flexible beading wire (2')
- Lobster claw clasp and jump ring
- Wire cutters

INSTRUCTIONS

1. Tape one end of flexible beading wire to work surface.

2. Pick up beads in random color and size order, using 6mm and 3.5mm round beads first.

Note: This is the area going around the back of the neck.

3. Approximately 5"–6" in, start adding spacer, art glass, and 6mm round beads. At approximately halfway point, add a spacer bead, one changeable bead bar, a spacer bead, one changeable bead bar, a spacer bead, and remaining changeable bead bar.

4. Unscrew the top (or in some designs the bottom) gold bar and add beads to fill the bars.

Note: Be certain to screw the ball back on tightly so you do not lose beads.

5. Add remaining beads in same pattern as first side.

Note: Look at the necklace. Because cellophane tape was used on the first end, additional beads can be added to each side or make changes before you finish the necklace by adding the clasp.

6. Attach lobster claw clasp and ring to the ends of the wire, using the crimps.

TIP:

Put extra beads in a small resealable bag, box them up, and give them as a gift with the necklace. The recipient can then change the bead bars as desired.

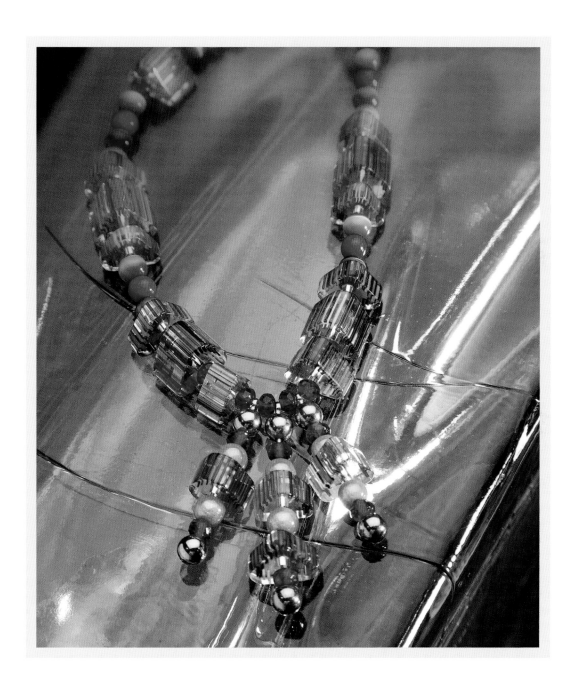

Crystal Hoop Earrings

Designed by Lisa Gettings

These large sparkly earrings are a big hit for any party or special occassion.

MATERIALS

- Beads:

    11/0 seed

    Czech fire-polished faceted rondelle (52)

- Ball post earrings (2)
- Chain-nosed pliers
- Heavy-duty wire cutters
- Memory wire
- Round-nosed pliers

INSTRUCTIONS

1. Cut one complete loop from memory wire spool. Fold over tip (2mm–3 mm) of wire, using the chain-nosed pliers to make a tiny flattened hook.

2. Add (1) purple rondelle, (1) seed, and (1) green rondelle beads. Continue this until approximately ¼" of wire is left to make a loop.

3. Bend wire to form a 90° angle, using the chain-nosed pliers. Hook earring finding onto memory wire and close loop, using round-nosed pliers.

TIP:

Memory wire is very stiff and difficult to bend. To make it easier to bend, you can pass a lighter over the wire and warm it up slightly; but if you get the wire too hot, it will become brittle and break. The best method is to warm it for just a second, hold one side close to the end with the chain-nosed pliers, then bend the tip with the other pliers. Go slowly! This wire responds best when you move it slowly.

Memory Wire Bracelet

This is a great bracelet to make with children as well as adults. It is very simple, very quick, and always fun! Your children can make them for their friends and family and give them with pride.

MATERIALS

- BEADS:

    Assorted

- Memory wire
- Round-nosed pliers
- Wire cutters

INSTRUCTIONS

1. Cut wire to desired size.

2. Bend one end of wire outward and around into a small circle, using round-nosed pliers. Refer to tip on bending memory wire on page 30.

Note: This is to keep the beads from falling off the end, and bending the wire in an outward manner will keep the wire from scratching the wrist.

3. Add beads as desired until only ½" wire remains.

Note: You can use almost any size beads; however, do not use anything smaller than an 11/0 seed bead.

4. Bend remaining end of wire outward and around into a small circle, using round-nosed pliers.

Variations: To make a triple-wrap bracelet as shown in top of photo above, follow the instructions for making a Memory Wire Bracelet at left, cutting enough wire to wrap around wrist three times. Add a charm before Step 4. To add space bars as shown in the bracelet at bottom of photo, cut two same-sized wire pieces and add beads with a space bar added every five beads.

Leather & Silver ID Bracelet

When my niece Emily was expecting her second little girl, she contemplated names like Madeline Elizabeth and Madeline Mae. A name that long will certainly be a bit difficult to put on a bracelet. So I propose, for all who want to do "name" bracelets, that initials might just work a bit better.

MATERIALS

- BEADS:

    5/0 seed (18)

    Initial

    Spacer or bali (16)

- Cord crimps (2)

- Flat-nosed pliers

- Leather cord

- Lobster claw clasp

- Split ring

INSTRUCTIONS

1. Cut cord to desired size.

2. Follow instructions for Cord Crimping on page 120 to attach crimp.

3. Pick up (9) black and (8) silver beads in an alternating pattern, ending with a black bead. String on silver initial beads followed by another set of (9) black and (8) silver beads in the same alternating pattern as the first side.

4. Attach remaining crimp to second end, following Cord Crimping instructions.

5. Attach lobster claw clasp onto the ring one end of the cord crimp. Attach the split ring to the remaining end.

Note: The braided bracelet shown in the right of the photo on page 35 was made by tripling the length of cord, braiding together, and adding a single charm.

TIP:

You can also use a ring barrel clasp as a closure for these bracelets by following the instructions for Barrel Clasp crimping on page 120.

Wavy Barrette

Designed by Lisa Gettings

These funky barrettes make great gifts for girls of all ages. Make a pair to match any outfit or any type of wardrobe.

MATERIALS

- BEADS:

    4mm or 6mm assorted glass

    11/0 or 13/0 seed

    Flat glass (9)

- 22-gauge sterling silver wire (1')
- Chain-nosed pliers
- E-6000 adhesive
- Flush-nosed cutters
- Metal barrette base
- Sandpaper

INSTRUCTIONS

1. Roughen up the barrette surface, using sandpaper.

2. Cover barrette surface and one side of each flat bead with thin layer of glue. Let all pieces cure 5–10 minutes.

3. Press beads onto barrette and let dry completely.

4. Fold 2mm–3mm tip of wire with flush cutters to make a tiny flattened hook.

5. Pick up (1) 4mm bead and take wire through first bead on the barrette. Pick up (4) seed, (1) 4mm glass, and (4) seed beads. Take wire down through next bead on barrette, allowing beads to form wave.

Part of the "charm" of charm bracelets is that they are easily personalized. Add charms that feature the recipient's favorite hobby, beads in their favorite colors, or a combination of both.

MATERIALS

- BEADS:

    3mm ball

    6mm flat spacer (2) per glass bead head pin

    Assorted

    Faceted glass

- 4mm open jump ring
- Chain
- Chain-nosed pliers
- Charms with jump rings
- Claw or toggle clasp
- Flush cutters
- Head pins
- Jump ring

INSTRUCTIONS

1. Cut chain to desired size.

2. Attach clasp to one end and jump ring to remaining end, using chain-nosed pliers.

3. Add charms 3–5 links apart.

Note: If you wish to make a very full bracelet, use a sturdier link and add as many charms and glass bead head pins as you want.

4. String ball, beads, and spacer beads onto head pins.

5. Attach head pins, using Bend-cut-curl Technique on page 120.

Intermediate
Beaded
Jewelry

Black & Gold Brick Stitch Earrings

This is a great quick gift. You can make a pair of these earrings in under a half hour. Make a few pair in a number of colors to give to coworkers and friends. I like to have a few of these on hand in black-and-silver, black-and-gold, and basic "denim friendly" colors for gift giving.

MATERIALS

- BEADS:

    2mm–3mm round

    11/0 seed

    Cube (28–30)

- Beading Notions on page 8
- Earring wires (2)

INSTRUCTIONS

1. Thread needle with 3' of thread. Begin base row, using Ladder Stitch on page 116.

2. Continue adding Rows 2–4, using Brick Stitch on page xx.

Note: Row 3 has (3) cubes and Row 4 has only (2) cubes.

3. To add earring wire, catch thread between Row 4 cubes and attach it to earring wire loop. Run needle and thread in and out of loop (4) times to secure.

Note: You can use French wire if it is available to you to hide the thread, or add a single cube before adding the ear wire.

4. To secure cubes in triangle, weave needle and thread up and down and back and forth as you head down to first cube in base row to add fringe.

5. To add fringe, exit first cube. Pick up fringe as shown in photo at right or in desired order. Be certain to anchor strand with a seed bead at bottom and take thread back up through the line.

6. Take needle and thread around (2) cubes to secure and move over to second cube.

Note: To make fringe angle, add (2) 3mm–4mm beads to begin and repeat the order as listed above.

> ### TIP:
> You can also make these earrings, using hex beads for a bit more dimension and a smaller triangle.

This stitch is the easiest and one of my favorites. When you do the square-stitch base with either cubes or large hex beads (the 8/0 delica beads work well too), you have a blank canvas. Follow the instructions below to create the Blue & Gold Triangle Bracelet shown below and at far right, then check out the instructions on page 44 to learn how to embellish the bracelets shown at right.

Blue & Gold Triangle Bracelet

MATERIALS

• BEADS:

   10/0 triangle (3–6 grams each of 2 colors)

   11/0 seed (for loop)

• Beading Notions on page 8

• Button

INSTRUCTIONS

1. Thread needle with at least 4' of thread and add a waste bead. Take stopper bead down to within 6" of thread end and run (2) slipknots around it.

Note: You can take the waste bead out anytime after 4–5 rows.

2. String rows, using Square Stitch on page 119 and following pattern at right.

Note: I like to work in the same direction as it is much easier. Just flip the piece after each row so you are always working from top to bottom.

3. To add button, stitch button onto one end by taking needle and thread in and out of two beads at end of center row at least four times to secure.

Note: You may want to pick up (2–3) seed beads before and after taking needle through button hole to cover any exposed thread.

4. To add button loop, exit one end of center bead at opposite end from button, pick up number of 11/0 seed beads that will comfortably fit around button.

Note: Be certain to run the needle and thread through the loop at least three times to secure.

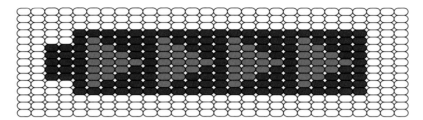

Blue & Gold Triangle Bracelet Pattern

Variations: See page 44 for instructions on each individual bracelet, all made with the Square Stitch technique.

Bracelets shown left to right in photo on page 43. For more details on making Embellishment Fringe, see page 121.

White & Red Square Stitch Bracelet

To make this bracelet, follow the instructions for Blue & Gold Triangle Bracelet on page 42 but use cube beads. If you are going to cover the entire top of the bracelet with a pattern, you can use any color cube.

I always tell my students that the cube base is a blank canvas; simply take the needle and thread out between two cubes and just do whatever you want. Start by taking your needle and thread up between two cubes and pick up (2-3) fringe beads. Go back down and over one cube. You can now do one of two things: 1. Cover all the cubes with fringe beads, or 2. Use a random pattern, covering the cubes.
Note: A fringe bead is a slightly oblong bead with a hole at the top.

Brown Bracelet with Crystal Cubes

To make a bracelet using crystal cubes, follow the instructions for making the Blue & Gold Triangle Bracelet on page 42. At Row 9, pick up cube as third and fourth beads from bottom of row.
Note: The space the cube takes up is (2) beads vertically and (2) beads horizontally, so you will also include cube in the next row in place of (2) triangles. Add a crystal cube every few rows.

Autumn-toned Bracelet

This bracelet is just a little trickier, so allow a few extra minutes and a little patience if this is your first time. Starting at one end and exiting between cubes, pick up (1) caramel-colored accent bead, then (1) 2mm round and (1) 11/0 seed beads to use as an anchor. Take needle and thread around seed bead and back up through the 2mm and the accent beads to hold them all in place.

Continue down bracelet, adding (1) accent, (1) 2mm round, and (1) 11/0 seed beads every few beads in somewhat of a wave pattern.

Remember, you can take the needle and thread anywhere you want by weaving through the cubes and exiting the place you want to add more beads.

After all accent beads have been added, add leaves.
Note: You can make leaf pieces as short or as long as you want. I suggest you keep it to (2–3) leaves per branch or you will have many loose, hanging pieces that you may not like.

Green & Gold Cube Bracelet

For this bracelet, complete cube base and exit needle and thread from last cube in row. Pick up (3) 10/0 or 11/0 seed beads, taking needle and thread across (1) cube and up (1) before going back up, causing beads to sit on a slight angle. Continue going up and down cube rows, adding seed beads. You can change the color of beads every other row as shown here or do them all in the same color.

Variation: If you have friends who are gardeners or love flowers, attach flowers to the base as shown above. For someone who loves the beach, add fish and shells.

Square Stitch Watch

These Square Stitch Watches make a perfect gift for the person who is always running a few minutes behind schedule. Make the band using any pattern desired such as the zigzag pattern shown in the black and gold watch or the random pattern in the blue and gold watch.

MATERIALS

- BEADS:

    11/0 seed (20–40, for loop closure)

    Cube (150)

- Beading Notions on page 8
- Button
- Watch face with removable bars

INSTRUCTIONS

1. Remove bars from both ends of watch face. Slide on cubes to cover bar and still be able to add bars back onto watch. Remove cubes and set aside.

2. Measure wrist and watch face.

Note: The easiest way to measure the wrist is to wrap a piece of ribbon around the wrist, cut it to size, and measure.

3. Subtract size of watch face from wrist size. Divide that number in half. The result is the size of each half of watchband. For example: If the wrist size measures 7" and the watch face measures 1½", the result is 5½". Half of 5½" is 2¾". Each watchband half should be 2¾".

4. Make each watchband half, following instructions for Square Stitch Bracelets on page 42, using width and length as determined in Step 3 above.

5. At end of each half, add cubes set aside in Step 1.

6. Slide watch bars into end of watchband and attach to watch face.

7. Add button and loop, following Steps 3–4 on page 42.

> **TIP:**
> If you have difficulty removing the watch bars with your fingers, try the small screwdriver from an eyeglass repair kit. It works great.

Use your imagination to embellish a Square Stitch Watch. This floral leaf pattern makes a great gift for your favorite gardener.

MATERIALS

- BEADS:

    8/0 seed (8 grams)

    11/0 seed

    15/0 seed

    Assorted flower (40–60)

    Cube (250–300)

    Fringe

- Beading Notions on page 8
- Button
- Large snap set
- Watch face with removable bars

INSTRUCTIONS

1. Follow instructions for Square Stitch Watch on page 46.

2. Bead a watch cover approximately 3" long and width of watchband, using 8/0 seed beads. Use either a square or peyote stitch to make cover. See Square Stitch on page 119 or Peyote Stitch on page 117.

3. Attach cover onto one end of watchband 3–4 rows from watch face.

4. Stitch half of snap onto cover bottom as shown in photo. Stitch second half onto watchband in appropriate place.

5. Add short leaf fringe over both sides of watchband and cover. Refer to Leaf Fringe on page 121. When adding fringe to second side of base, stop a few rows before the snap to allow for clasp.

    Note: Every so often, close cover to make certain it still lies correctly over watch.

6. Add flowers onto band. Coming out between cubes, pick up (1) flower bead, then (1) fringe or 15/0 seed bead to anchor flower into place. Add as many or as few flowers as desired.

    Note: I always add my flowers last, that way if I have any sparse areas, I can fill in with flowers.

7. Add button and loop, following Steps 3–4 for Square Stitch Bracelets on page 42.

Cubist Barrette

Designed by Lisa Gettings

These barrettes are another way to use the square stitch. Make them in different color combinations for girls of all ages.

MATERIALS

- BEADS:

    4mm multicolored miyuki cube

- Beading Notions on page 8
- E-6000 adhesive
- Flush cutters
- Metal barrette base
- Sandpaper

INSTRUCTIONS

1. Follow instructions for Square Stitch on page 119 to make a square-stitched strip 21 rows long and 4–5 rows wide. Add beads randomly or establish a pattern.

2. Roughen surface of the metal barrette base, using sandpaper.

Note: This will help the glue adhere better.

3. Spread a thin, even layer of glue onto barrette base and one side of square-stitched strip. Let pieces cure for 5–10 minutes.

4. Press barrette and strip together and let dry completely.

Note: Scrape off the excess glue from the inside of barrette before wearing.

TIP:
When gluing the finished square stitch piece to the barrette base, clamp it on each end with two small binder clips until dry.

Bugle beads are so beautiful and so under used. It took me a few tries, but I finally came up with these terrific bracelets.

Black & Gold Bracelet

MATERIALS

- BEADS:

    1/4" bugle (250–300)

    12/0 Charlotte (4–6 grams)

- Beading Notions on page 8
- Button

Instructions

1. Thread needle with 4' thread.

2. Pick up (2) bugle beads and take down to within 6"–8" of thread end. Make Row 1 length of wrist, using Ladder Stitch on page 116.

Note: Row 1 will be center row.

3. Coming out top of last bugle bead in "center row", pick up (2) bugle beads and slide them to sit on top of the bugle bead exited on center row. Take needle and thread and catch thread between last two bugle beads in center row. Continue across entire row, using Brick Stitch on page 116.

4. Take needle and thread down through both rows and work brick stitch across the third row.

Note: They will not line up exactly but will slightly jut in on one end and out on the other.

5. To embellish bracelet top, come out first bead at beginning of top row. Create picots, following Picot Edging instructions on page 9, using Charlotte beads. Add them to both outside rows.

6. Add picots to outside edge of center row.

Note: These picots will stand up instead of out, creating a smaller look to the center row.

7. Add button and loop, following Steps 3–4 for Square Stitch Bracelet on page 42.

TIP:

Go through your bugle beads before you begin and weed out the shorter ones and any with sharp edges as the sharp edges cut your thread.

Variations: To create the embellishment on the center bracelet, when coming out of the last bugle beads added, pick up (6) Charlotte beads. Then go around and back through the same bugle bead, allowing the seed beads to sit on top of the bugle bead. Continue across row, adding the Charlotte beads in the same manner to cover the bugle beads. Create a wavy pattern by picking up (5) orange and (1) raspberry beads. Continue to add beads, staggering the raspberry bead that will create a wavy pattern. The same was done with the blue bracelet, except an antique-gold Charlotte bead was added to create the wave.

Bundle of Beads

This technique has to be my all-time favorite. It is a great way to use up a leftover stash of beads. Gather colors that work well together, dump them into a bowl, and get started. If you are a lampwork artist and wish to give your work as gifts, try this technique and showcase your piece in the center. This is also a wonderful way to make a bracelet to match a sweater or shirt.

MATERIALS

- BEADS:

    6/0 seed

    11/0 seed (assorted round, square and disc-shaped)

    Large focal (optional)

    Small focal

- Beading Notions on page 8
- Crimping tool or flat-nosed pliers
- Crimps (2)
- Flexible beading wire
- Toggle clasp

INSTRUCTIONS

1. Cut a piece of wire to desired length plus 2".

2. Attach one toggle piece, using crimps.

Note: Be certain there is at least ¼" tail to cover with beads before crimping closed.

3. Pick up (4–6) 6/0 seed beads and (1–3) small focal beads. Repeat pattern to desired length.

Notes: If you want a center focal bead, string it on at the halfway point. Periodically try it around the wrist to see where the center point falls, or use a strip of ribbon to measure the wrist and hold against that for sizing.

4. End piece with set of 6/0 seed beads. Attach remaining toggle clasp, using crimp.

5. Thread needle with (1) 11/0 stopper bead.

6. Take needle and thread through first 6/0 seed bead (either side) and begin to embellish using one of the embellishment techniques for Leaf Fringe, Stick Fringe, Loops, or Straight Small Line Embellishments on page 121.

7. Add embellishments between each 6/0 seed bead. Fill each 6/0 seed bead four-bead section by moving back and forth until it is embellished as desired. Take needle and thread through focal bead and continue embellishing on remaining side.

8. When finished, weave thread through a number of embellishment sections to secure, then snip off the excess thread. Repeat with beginning thread.

I love doing the peyote stitch. I do not, however, like those little amulet bags some people like, as I find them too cumbersome. So instead of beading around a paper towel roll, I decided to bead around aquarium tubing to make a choker piece, leaving the tubing in and using the tubing connectors as my clasp.

MATERIALS

- BEADS:

    3mm firepolish crystal

    Crystal (4–5)

    Delica (10–15 grams)

    Large crystal spacer (3) (optional)

    Small crystal spacer (10)

    Small round or crystals (10)

- ⅛"-diameter aquarium tubing (16")

- 1½"-diameter plastic ring

- Beading Notions on page 8

- Tubing connector

- Wooden skewer

INSTRUCTIONS

1. Insert wooden skewer into tube to keep it straight and stiff while working.

2. Cover entire tube, using Tubular Peyote Stitch on page 117.

3. Follow Steps 1–5 for Tubular Peyote Stitch to cover ring.

4. Remove wooden skewer and insert tube connector into one end to act as clasp.

5. Make a peyote bale, using the Flat Peyote Techinque below. When you connect the plastic ring to the tubing, be certain the flat peyote ends fit together before weaving them closed.

6. To create fringe, pick up (2) seed, (1) 3mm fire-polish crystal, (1) small fire-polish spacer, (1) slightly larger fire-polish spacer, (1) small spacer crystal, (1) large spacer, (1) small spacer, (1) 3mm round, (1) 3mm fire-polish crystal, and (3) seed beads to complete picot anchor.

7. Take needle and thread back through line and continue weaving around and back down at least (3) times to secure thread.

Note: You can do an occasional slipknot between the beads for additional security. Add two more fringe lines with the middle one slightly longer by adding an additional larger crystal and another small crystal spacer as shown in photo at right.

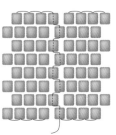

Flat Peyote Technique

Flat-backed Cabochon

This technique is wonderful and can make any number of beaded objects. This cabochon works great as a pin or necklace bale. Lacey's Stiff Stuff® is the only material I use for backing. It is readily available in most bead stores, craft stores, and on-line. Ultrasuede or leather may work for you, but I prefer Stiff Stuff.

MATERIALS

- BEADS:

    8/0 seed (3 grams)

    11/0 seed (3 grams)

- Beading Notions on page 8
- E-6000 adhesive
- Flat-backed cabochon
- Leather or ultrasuede backing
- Stiff Stuff® (2)
- Pin with barrel backing

INSTRUCTIONS

1. Glue cabochon onto matte Stiff Stuff. Let dry a few hours.

2. Trim backing, leaving a ⅛"– ¼" border around cabochon.

3. Thread needle with 3'–4' thread and knot at bottom. Beginning in back, take needle out as close to cabochon as possible.

4. Pick up (3) 8/0 seed beads. Take needle and thread down through backing and back up between the second and third beads just added.

Note: Be certain to lay beads as close to cabochon edge as possible.

5. Take needle and thread through third bead and continue picking up (3) 8/0 seed beads at a time, going around the piece until you reach the end.

6. Take needle and thread through all 8/0 seed beads just added to straighten and give piece extra security.

7. Using 11/0 seed beads, co the Peyote Stitch on page 117 to add beads up and over cabochon.

Note: I suggest you do no more than three rows around both sections. The exception is if you have a very large cabochon and need to build up around the piece more than three rows will allow. You can also do a small ruffle on the outside edge by picking up (3) 11/0 seed beads instead of (1) when doing your peyote stitch.

8. To finish the piece, when all the beads have been added, take needle and thread out through back. Knot and snip off excess thread. Trim any edge of backing that is still showing when looking at piece from the front.

9. Lay pin back on backing piece halfway up and mark (2) holes on either end of the leather or suede backing where pin will come through. Cut a small slit and push the pin through to the outside. Trim leather backing to fit, then glue onto back, covering all threads.

Note: If you are using a pin back with a bale, be certain to cut a slit for the bale piece as well. Add glue to both the thread backing and pin and cover and glue in place. Trim away any excess. If backing can still be seen around the outside edges, stitch around the two where necessary.

I love doing this technique, as it is very simple and fairly fast. I can do one using all the same size beads in the loop and watch a movie at the same time. The following instructions are for the bracelet. To make the necklace, just use a longer wire.

Loopty Doo Bracelet

MATERIALS

- BEADS:

    3mm–6mm round

    8/0 seed (7–10 grams)

    10/0 Czech seed (1 hank)

    11/0 seed (4–6 grams)

    Focal (optional)

    Spacer

- Beading Notions on page 8
- Crimping tool or flat-nosed pliers
- Crimps (4)
- Toggle clasp or lobster claw clasp and jump ring

INSTRUCTIONS

1. Cut wire to desired length plus 1". Attach first clasp piece on one end, using crimp.

2. Pick up (6) 8/0 seed and (3) 3mm–6mm round beads. Continue pattern until wire is full.

3. Add the remaining clasp piece, using crimp, running ½" excess wire through the final few beads for additional security.

4. To add loops, add (1) 11/0 stopper bead. Be certain to leave at least a 6" tail that you will weave in later. Take needle and thread through first seed bead.

Note: Use as much thread as you feel comfortable working with. I suggest at least 3'–6'. Remember, the more thread you use, the less new thread you will have to add.

5. Pick up (3) 10/0 seed, (3) 11/0 seed, (3) 10/0 seed, (3) 11/0 seed, (3) 10/0 seed, (1) 2mm–6mm round, (3) 10/0 seed, (3) 11/0 seed, (3) 10/0 seed, (3) 11/0 seed, and (3) 10/0 seed beads.

6. Take needle and thread back through the same spot and over (1) bead in base. This completes first loop. Continue across bracelet base, adding loops in same manner or alternating loop sizes and bead order as desired.

Note: For the necklace, choose a focal bead and add additional 10/0 and 11/0 seed beads and round beads into the loop section.

If you need a gift in a hurry and you want to do some form of beadweaving, this is the one to do. The bigger the beads you use, the faster it goes. I love using the cubes with the 8/0 seed beads to give the piece dimension.

MATERIALS

- BEADS:

    8/0 seed (10 grams)

    11/0 seed (20 grams)

- Beading Notions on page 8
- Toggle clasp

INSTRUCTIONS

1. Pick up (4) 8/0 seed and (4) 11/0 seed beads. Take them down to within 6" of thread end.

2. Follow instructions for Spiral Rope on page 118 to complete necklace.

3. Stitch on toggle closure by picking up (2–3) seed beads, go through loop end and another (2–3) seed beads, and back throgh end of piece. Repeat 3–4 times to secure.

Variations: Different looks can be achieved by using the Spiral Rope Technique and different-sized beads. To create the brown spiral rope necklace and bracelet above, continue using 8/0 seed beads for the core, but switch to (1) 8/0 seed, (1) cube, and (1) 8/0 seed beads for the outside spiral. You can vary the colors of the cubes in an every-other pattern or use the same color. Or, use gold 8/0 seed beads and black cubes for a dressier look.

Easy
Accessories
and Decor

Beaded Button Napkin Rings

Designed by Lisa Gettings

These napkin rings are a unique gift. Give them as a gift, wrapped around linen napkins.

MATERIALS

- BEADS:

    11/0 or larger seed

    Faceted rondelle

    Faceted round

- 2-hole buttons
- Beading Notions on page 8
- Carpet thread
- Hair elastics
- Sewing needle
- Strong thread

INSTRUCTIONS

1. Double-thread needle, then knot. Take thread through hair elastic and up through one hole in button.

2. Pick up (1) seed, (1) rondelle, (1) seed, (1) rondelle, and (1) seed beads. Bring needle back down through beads to anchor and bring needle out through button back.

3. Wind thread around and through elastic and secure button to it. Bring needle up through second buttonhole and repeat Step 2.

4. Wind thread around and through elastic a couple of times to secure button in place.

5. Knot off thread and cut.

Note: To make a napkin ring using a 4-holed button such as the brown buttons shown in photo at right, add beads and take the needle down through hole diagonal from starting point. Then come up through an empty hole. Add remaining beads and take down through final hole.

TIP:
Follow these instructions to create colorful ponytail holders that girls of any age would enjoy receiving as a gift.

Beaded Jar Candle

Party guests and hostesses alike appreciate receiving a party favor or thank-you gift. I particularly love giving my guests a little something to remember our gathering. These beaded jar candles are an easy and inexpensive idea.

MATERIALS

- BEADS:
    Assorted
- Candle with lid
- Charms
- Craft glue
- Stretch cord

INSTRUCTIONS

1. Cut cord to desired size.

2. Follow instructions for Red and Black Stretch Cord Bracelets on page 16, stringing beads and charms randomly onto stretch cord.

3. Slip beads over candle lid.

TIP:

Gold and crystal beads and charms work well for a New Year's Eve party favor, while aquatic charms make the candle a wonderful hostess gift for a pool party.

Each year my family has a summer party and I make my own party favors. Last year I made this visor for each lady in attendance. This visor would also make a great gift for any outdoor-loving friend.

MATERIALS

- BEADS:

    Fringe

- Beading Notions on page 8
- Decorative puckered ribbon
- Craft glue
- Visor

INSTRUCTIONS

1. Cut ribbon to fit around visor brim.

2. Thread needle and come out the front of the ribbon at one end. Pick up (3) fringe beads and take needle back down at beginning point.

Note: This will make the fringe beads pucker and look like a small flower.

3. Continue down the entire ribbon, adding (3) fringe beads randomly until the end is reached.

4. Knot thread and glue decorative ribbon on visor.

Lacey Hatband

My sister Nancy, my mother and myself spend summers at the beach. It's become tradition to come up with a new beach hat for each season.

MATERIALS

- BEADS:

    Fringe

- Beading Notions on page 8
- Lace (4')
- Ribbon (4')
- Straw hat

INSTRUCTIONS

1. Tie the lace around the hat, leaving a 1' tail on each side of knot.

2. Thread needle and knot thread. Pick up (3) drop beads at a time and attach each set to ribbon approximately ¼" apart.

3. Once the entire ribbon is beaded, gently pull remaining thread to pleat ribbon.

4. Wrap ribbon around hat and tack every ½" or so on the inside of the hat.

Do you have a family member or friend who belongs to the Red Hat Society? Here is a fun gift idea.

MATERIALS

- BEADS:

    11/0 seed

    Large drop

- 1½"-wide white wire-edged ribbon

- Beading Notions on page 8

- E-6000 adhesive

- Stiff Stuff® (see page 58)

- Silk leaves

- Silk poppies (6–8)

- Straw hat

INSTRUCTIONS

1. Measure hatband. Cut a piece of ribbon twice the length of the headband.

2. Gently pull the wires on both sides of the ribbon to create a pleating effect. Attach the ribbon to the hat by tying a knot in the two wire ends and trimming off excess ribbon and wire.

3. Take the poppies apart and discard the stem.

Note: Keep the leaves to glue on randomly around the flowers.

4. Place two poppy pieces onto a small piece of Stiff Stuff. Add (1) drop bead at a time to attach poppy pieces and drops to Stiff Stuff.

Note: If the drop beads have a hole in the top and bottom, anchor each with an 11/0 seed bead.

5. Trim the Stiff Stuff so it cannot be seen when the flower is glued onto the hat.

6. Repeat Steps 3–5 to create 3–4 more beaded flowers.

7. Glue leaves and flowers onto hat, covering the knot made in the ribbon hatband.

I love the look of embroidery but am a terrible sketcher. So as usual, I found a fun shortcut that is fairly quick, using either a rubber stamp or a stencil. You can give an evening bag such as this one as a gift for any age. It can be used for any special evening occasion so make one to match a prom dress, bridesmaid attire, or any other event you can think of.

MATERIALS

- BEADS:

    11/0 seed (for leaves and stem)

    Fringe
- Beading Notions on page 8
- Flower stencil
- Satin evening bag
- Stenciling pencils

INSTRUCTIONS

1. Position stencil and color lightly onto bag.

Note: If the bag has a lining, open it up enough to comfortably be able to get your fingers in to hold the material. Sew it closed after beading is finished.

2. Thread needle and make a knot in the end. Take needle and thread out from the back, exiting along the stencil's outside edge. Pick up (3) fringe beads, lining them up along the outside edge of the stenciled pattern, stitching back down through the fabric and back up and out between Beads 2 and 3. Take needle and thread through the third fringe bead.

3. Pick up another (3) beads, continuing around the outside edges of the pattern and using this same method.

Note: You can also use the couching stitch or any other stitch you may be comfortable using.

4. Fill in the red flower area. Pick up (3) fringe beads at a time and take needle and thread around and around into the middle of each section of the stencil until all pencil markings are covered.

5. Fill in the small green leaf sections. Pick up enough 11/0 seed beads to fill the space from top to bottom, tacking the rows down every (2–3) beads.

TIP:
Anything you can trace around works great. For example, trace around a small star-shaped cookie cutter and fill in with gold beads.

Beach Glass Centerpiece

I love the beach and I love collecting beach glass and shells. However, finding a creative use has always been a challenge. This colorful centerpiece is one that will brighten any table.

MATERIALS

- BEADS:

    Assorted

- 14-gauge wire
- 20- or 24-gauge wire
- Beach glass
- Head pins
- Stand for hanging glass

INSTRUCTIONS

1. Cut (2) 6" pieces of 20- or 24-gauge wire.

2. Hold the pieces of wire together and wrap around beach glass, ending with the wire at the top.

3. Trim wire end to 1"–2".

4. Weave one wire around the other a few times and back down the glass.

5. Make a loop on wire's second end, using round-nosed pliers.

6. To add bottom beads, shape wire into a figure 8. Attach one end to bottom of wire-wrapped bead.

7. Add beads onto head pin and use Bend-cut-curl Technique or page 120 to attach onto bottom of the figure 8.

TIP:
If your beach glass has sharp edges, be sure to sand them down with medium-weight sandpaper before you begin.

Swiss Dot Lamp Shade

Designed by Lisa Gettings

I have always loved the clean delicate look of Swiss dot fabric. Inspired by that design idea, I created this sweet little shade for a lamp I have next to my bed. The light shines through the transparent glass beads, adding a warm glow to the room.

MATERIALS

- BEADS:

    Delica (8 grams)

    Multicolored Czech pressed-glass spacer (2–3 strands)

- 4"–6"-tall lamp shade
- Beading Notions on page 8
- Decorative trim or ribbon
- Double-sided beading tape
- Fine Fireline beading thread
- Flush cutters
- Heavy-duty sewing needle

INSTRUCTIONS

1. Pierce small holes all over lamp shade, using heavy-duty sewing needle.

Note: Make certain to keep them as small as possible by not pushing the needle all the way through.

2. Thread the beading needle with 4' of thread and add a stopper bead at one end. Thread the needle through the first hole from inside to outside, anchoring the stopper bead.

3. Pick up (1) spacer and (1) delica beads and position the spacer flat against the surface of the shade with the delica on top.

4. Go back through the hole in the spacer and the hole in the shade, anchoring beads.

5. Take needle through the next closest hole and add a delica. Go back through the shade.

6. Repeat Steps 3–5 until all holes are beaded.

Note: If you run out of thread, knot the end at the top or bottom of the shade. Then follow Step 2 to add thread.

7. Measure top and bottom of shade.

8. Cut trim to fit bottom and top of shade, then adhere with beading tape.

Note: You may be able to see the thread slightly through the shade, depending on the color of the shade, but it doesn't deter from the overall look. I used this beading thread, as opposed to an invisible fishing line or other such thread, because it must be extremely durable and hold up to the heat of a lightbulb.

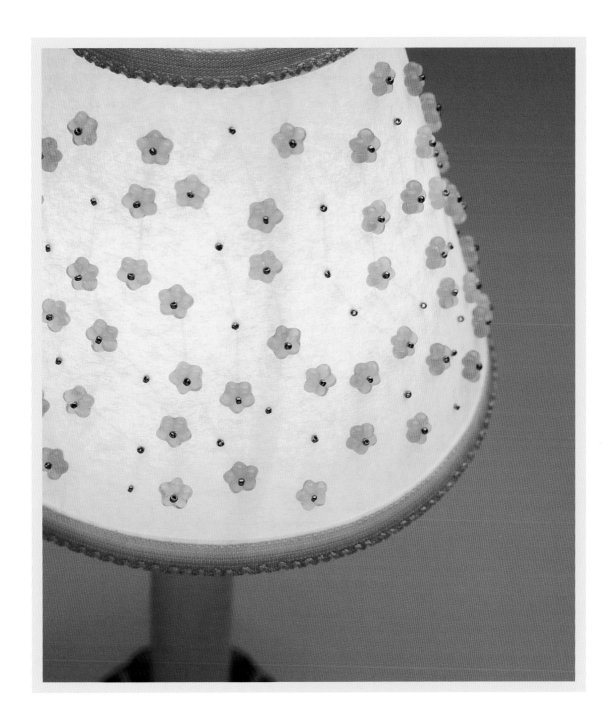

Intermediate
Accessories
and Decor

Beaded Fringe Lamp Shade

I love beautiful lamp shades, especially the ones with beaded fringing. However, it never fails that the styles I really like have the wrong color of beads. That is when I decided to make my own to coordinate with my room.

MATERIALS

- BEADS:

   3mm fire-polish (15–18)

   6mm faceted flat spacer (75–100)

   6mm round (28)

   11/0 seed (3-4 grams)

   15/0 seed (50)

- 4"–6" tall satin-embossed lamp shade
- Beading Notions on page 8
- Decorative trim
- Pencil

INSTRUCTIONS

1. Measure around lamp shade bottom. Using a pencil, make small dots where fringe will be added.

Note: My lamp shade measured 15" around the bottom. I marked every 1" so that I would have 15 equally spaced fringes.

2. Thread 4' of thread onto needle and knot bottom.

3. Take needle through material edge at first pencil mark.

Note: Thread should not go from outside to inside of shade, but should run around the inside.

4. Pick up (3–5) 11/0 seed beads.

Note: These beads will be covered by trim, so be certain to add enough so that the larger bead is not covered by trim.

5. Pick up beads as desired or alternate colors when stringing. For this shade, add (3) 6mm spacer, (1) 6mm round, (2) 6mm spacer, (3) 15/0 seed beads.

6. Make a picot at end with the final seed beads and take the thread back through the line of beads. See Picot Edging on page 9.

7. At top of fringe, catch a small amount of edge material and make a slipknot.

8. Repeat Steps 4–7 until all pencil marks are covered by fringe. After completing last fringe, knot thread.

9. Cut trim to fit shade bottom. Glue trim around bottom of shade to cover pencil marks and thread.

Beaded Ornament

The first time I made one of these ornaments and had to take it off the tree and put it away for the season, I nearly cried. That's when I decided to make one, take the top hook off, turn it upside down, and place it in a brass candleholder in my bay window. I now get to look at my lovely designs all year long. Make one of these for yourself and a friend, and show them how they can keep theirs out all year, too.

MATERIALS

- Beads:

    4mm faceted round crystal (31)

    6mm faceted round crystal (70)

    8mm x 10mm faceted oval crystal (10)

    11/0 seed (5 grams)

- Beading Notions on page 8
- Clear Christmas ball

INSTRUCTIONS

1. To make top circle, thread your needle with 4' thread. Pick up (1) 6mm round crystal and (2) 11/0 seed beads. Repeat until (33) beads are strung.

2. Tie into a circle. Make certain thread exits circle through the first crystal.

3. To create the loops, pick up (5) 11/0 seed, (1) 6mm round crystal, (5) 11/0 seed, (1) 4mm round crystal, (5) 11/0 seed, (1) 4mm round crystal, (5) 11/0 seed, (1) 6mm round crystal, (5) 11/0 seed beads.

4. Take the thread back up through the wire to the last 4mm crystal in the line. Pick up (5) 11/0 seed beads and go through the next crystal round in the line. Continue to the top.

5. Take needle and thread through the next crystal in the circle and repeat Step 3 around the entire circle.

6. To connect the loops, take needle and thread down to the bottom of first loop, exiting out the bottom 6mm crystal. Pick up (5) 11/0 seed, (1) 4mm round crystal, and (5) 11/0 seed beads.

7. Take needle and thread over to the next long loop and repeat Step 6 until all of the loops are connected.

8. To add the fringe, exit first 4mm round crystals at the bottom of the long loops. Pick up (5) 11/0 seed beads, (1) 4mm round, (5) 11/0 seed, (1) 4mm round, (5) 11 seed, (1) 4mm round, (1) 10mm x 8mm crystal, (1) 4mm round, and (1) 11/0 seed beads to anchor the line.

9. Take needle and thread around the last 11/0 seed bead and up through all the beads to the first 4mm round bead in the line. Pick up (5) 11/0 seed beads and take needle and thread over to the next 4mm round crystal, then repeat Step 8, adding fringe all the way around the bottom of the piece.

Note: You will need to manipulate your piece or hang it over your Christmas ball to finish the last few fringes. To secure start and finish threads, weave through piece, up and down and in and out until it is secure. Snip threads to finish. See alternate photo on page 128.

Beaded Mirror with Leather Case

Similar to beading around a cabochon, this beaded mirror is another example of this technique. You can bead around almost anything that has a fairly flat back.

MATERIALS

- BEADS:

    11/0 seed

- 2" x 3" or purse-sized oval mirror
- Beading Notions on page 8
- E-6000
- Leather elbow patch
- Stiff Stuff® (see page 58)

INSTRUCTIONS

1. Follow Steps 1–8 for Flat-backed Cabochon on page 58.

2. Create Picot Edging along the outside edge, using instructions on page 9.

Note: To make a purse case to hold the mirror, create a picot, using (1) 11/0 seed, (1) 8/0 seed, and (1) 11/0 seed beads in the front and back of each hole in the patches. Notes: The beauty of leather elbow patches is that they already have holes in them. Be certain to leave enough space for the beaded mirror to slide easily into the case.

Blue & Green Fringe Scarf Pin

See close-up of pin on page 80.

I just learned to knit and I am having a ball combining knitting and beading. As I run around at work, my scarves and shawls tend to slide off or to the side. I was trying to come up with a pin idea by looking at all the different pin components at the bead shop and happened to glance at the component for making a barrette. No sharp edges, holds in hair (or in this case, bulky yarn) what more could I ask for.

MATERIALS

- BEADS:

    11/0 seed

    Fringe (7 grams)

- Barrette finding
- Beading Notions on page 8

INSTRUCTIONS

1. Following instructions for Tubular Peyote Stitch on page 117, cover barrette top from left to right. Cover as much as possible while still being able to close barrette.

2. Take needle and thread through first seed bead. Pick up (2–3) fringe beads.

3. Weave through every other seed bead until barrette top is covered.

Note: Be careful not to weave fringe beads too close to inner edges. Close barrette every so often to be certain you have not overembellished.

Make these pieces to give together or on separate occasions. Either way, these pieces will complement any ensemble.

Scarf Pin

MATERIALS

- BEADS:

    8/0 seed

    Drop or fringe

- Beading Notions on page 8
- Dichroic glass
- E-6000 adhesive
- Flat–backed cabochon
- Leather or ultrasuede backing
- Stiff Stuff® (2) (see page 58)
- Pin with barrel backing

INSTRUCTIONS

1. Following the instructions for Flat-backed Cabochon on page 58, using a piece of dichroic glass to bead around.

2. To add dimension to glass, add fringe or drop beads for the last round going on the top.

Note: I also used single-leaf fringe on the outside edge in layers to add dimension. To make Leaf Fringe, see instructions on page 121, using as few or as many colors that work with the piece of dichroic glass.

To make this beaded hatband using a garter stitch, string on beads (5/0 triangles work best) before you begin knitting. The hatband takes approximately 20–30 grams of beads, depending on how beady you want the piece. Pull up a bead per stitch every other row. Try the hatband around the hat you intend to wear it with, as all hats and bands are slightly different. When fit becomes snug, cast off and stitch the ends together. To create this beaded scarf, either make or purchase a scarf with long fringe. Using a large-eyed needle, pick up (3–4) 5/0 triangle beads randomly onto the fringe and tie a slipknot.

To create this beaded scarf, either make or purchase a scarf with long fringe. Using a large-eyed needle, pick up (3–4) 5/0 triangle beads randomly onto the fringe and tie a slipknot.

I love wearing my knitted scarfs and shawls out and about, but hate to be constantly adjusting them. A beaded stickpin just didn't work for some of my more lightweight pieces. I was watching my daughter put her hair up in one of her many clips when it hit me: lightweight, no sharp points, and easy to bead to match my pieces.

MATERIALS

- BEADS:

    11/0 seed (10 grams)

    Assorted round and crystal

- Barrette finding
- Beading Notions on page 8

INSTRUCTIONS

1. Following instructions fro Tubular Peyote Stitch on page 117, cover barrette top from left to right. Cover as much as possible while still being able to close barrette.

2. Take needle and thread out through the seed bead on top-left edge. Pick up (3) seed beads and take through next seed bead. Add ruffled picot edge.

    Note: This will cause the (3) new seed beads to buckle, curve, and make a wavy picot edge.

3. Continue going up and down the outside edges and the ends to cover all the barrette parts seen from the front.

4. To add dangles, exit bottom edge far left and pick up (2–3) 11/0 seed and (3–4) round beads. Anchor by picking up (3) 11/0 seed beads and going back up through row of fringe.

    Note: Be certain that the (3) anchor beads form a picot before moving over a few beads and continuing your fringing.

Variation: Beaded shawl pins also make fabulous embellishments or drapery tie-backs.

Beaded Fringe Vase Collars

Adding this bead fringe to a plain glass vase is a great way to dress up any home decor.

MATERIALS

- BEADS:
    - 8/0 seed
    - 11/0 seed
    - Assorted flower
- Beading Notions on page 8
- Glass bowl or vase with lip
- Heavy-duty wire cutters
- Memory wire
- Round-nosed pliers

INSTRUCTIONS

1. Cut memory wire to size of vase neck. Using pliers, make round loop at one end.

2. Add enough 8/0 seed beads to cover wire. Make round loop at second end for hanging bead fringe.

3. Thread needle and add a stopper bead, leaving a 6" tail to weave in later.

4. Take needle and thread in (1) 8/0 seed bead and out between the next. Begin adding 11/0 seed beads to the desired fringe length. Secure this line by taking needle and thread around the last bead added and up through the second to last bead.

5. Begin adding Leaf Fringe as shown on page 121 up the line, adding (3) flower "bunches." Add as many leaf fringe strands as desired.

Note: I covered the wire loop ends with flowers and 11/0 seed beads, but the whole thing can be removed and worn as a bracelet.

The first time I ever saw a beaded piece was an amulet bag done in flat peyote, and I was sure I would never be able to learn how to do such an intricate stitch. It is not the easiest or the quickest, but it is certainly very rewarding when you finish a piece using delica beads.

Love You Bookmark
MATERIALS

- BEADS:

    3mm crystal (6)

    11/0 delica (10 grams, in 2 colors)

    12mm heart (3–4)

- Beading Notions on page 8
- Love You Bookmark Pattern

INSTRUCTIONS

1. Thread needle and add waste bead, leaving 6" tail.

Note: These rows will be removed when you have finished your design. It is easier to get a pattern started if you have something to hold on to and "waste rows" work great.

2. Pick up (10) 11/0 delica beads in background color and do 3 or 4 solid rows using Peyote Technique on page 117.

3. Follow Love You Bookmark pattern at right.

4. Remove rows added in Step 2 above.

5. Add hearts and 3mm crystals to the ends of piece, burying any loose threads.

Love You Bookmark Pattern

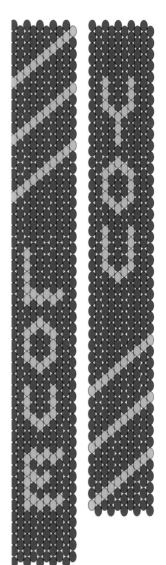

Variation: To make this diagonal-striped bookmark, create a diagonal pattern on the Peyote Graph on page 122 and use black and gold beads. Refer to Peyote Stitch on page 117.

Variation: The Beaded Bookmark technique on page 96 also makes a great bracelet. Just skip adding the fringed ends, add a button and loop, and you have a great piece of "wrist art."

When I got my new couch a few weeks before Christmas, I decided to make matching throw pillows with some contrasting fabric. I still had a little bit of fabric left, so I decided to make these cute stockings to hang on my tree. These ornaments make great gifts for friends, just select colors that coordinate with their room.

MATERIALS

• BEADS:

> Coordinating

• 12"-square fabric piece

• Beading Notions on page 8

• Fabric scissors

• Iron

• Lace or ribbon edging (optional for cuff)

• Pencil

• Star charms

• Tassels and cord (optional)

• Tracing paper

INSTRUCTIONS

1. Enlarge the Stocking Pattern below to desired size and cut out.

2. Fold fabric in half, pin, and cut out the stocking. With right sides facing, sew the stocking together with either a sewing machine or freehand, allowing ½" at the top to fold under.

3. Turn stocking right side out, fold top under, and press with iron.

4. To attach tassels, stitch cord to outside corner of stocking.

Note: If using lace or ribbon, pin in position and loosely stitch onto the stocking.

5. Knot a long piece of beading thread and come out the back of the tassel knot and begin adding beads and spacers in an alternating pattern ending with a small star charm.

Note: You can make as many strands as you like but remember, you don't want the stocking to be too heavy as this will make it difficult to hang on a tree. I added a little beaded loop from left to right, as this section seemed too bare without a few beads.

You can stitch a loop onto the left corner or use a Christmas ornament hook twisted into the lace. I have used both methods.

Stocking Pattern

(Enlarge as desired or trace a purchased stocking you have on hand.)

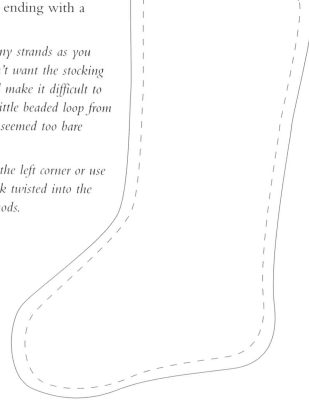

Variation: To embellish with beads and wire, as shown in the left and right stockings, sew on leaf beads in a circle, using seed beads to anchor. Add several larger round beads in the center. If desired, thread curly wire through the beads.

I love making beaded tassels. I give them as gifts or hang them from a wrapped gift box. I have approximately 40 hanging around my house.

Black, White & Carmel Tassel

MATERIALS

- BEADS:

  3mm fire-polish (100)

  11/0 seed

- Beading Notions on page 8

- Premade tassel

INSTRUCTIONS

1. Tubular-peyote-stitch around the neck of the tassel for approximately 6–7 rows, using seed beads. See Tubular Peyote Stitch, on page 117.

2. Begin making a ruffle edge along both the top and bottom edges of the tubular peyote by picking up (3) 11/0 seed beads between every (2) seed beads.

Note: You can do a second ruffle row and add the small fire-polish crystals. Pick up (1) 11/0 seed, (1) small crystal, and the remaining 11/0 seed beads instead of (3) 11/0 seed beads.

3. To add large loops, exit a seed bead along the inner bottom row and pick up (60) seed beads, alternating colors and fire-polish crystals every few beads.

4. Take your needle out and thread through the seed bead next to the one that began the loop. Move all the way around the tassel neck, adding loops in this manner.

5. (Optional) Add a circle of beads at the topknot of the tassel, using 11/0 seed and fire-polish beads and weaving into the tassel threads to secure.

Red Tassel
MATERIALS

• BEADS:

Assorted seed

• ½"-wide seam binding or ¼"-wide ribbon

• Beading Notions on page 8

INSTRUCTIONS

1. Make bead soup by emptying leftover or favorite beads into bowl.

2. To make the base, roll binding or ribbon to form a neck base approximately ⅛"–½" thick.

3. Thread needle and knot end. Run thread through roll horizontally to hold roll together. Loop thread around bottom of roll and come out top.

4. Pick up (12–14) seed beads and take the needle in the bottom of the binding or ribbon and back up and down. Picking up seed beads and cover the roll all the way around.

Note: If you have some ribbon showing along the bottom edge, don't worry—you will not see it when you add your loops. If you see ribbon showing along the top, pick up a few seed beads and cover the area.

5. To add the hanging loop, exit through the top middle of roll and add a few larger beads and (40–50) seed beads to make top loop.

6. Take needle and thread around and back down through the larger beads.

7. To add the loops, follow Step 3 of Black, White, & Carmel Tassel on page 102.

Linda's Gallery

"Fringe Frenzy" (flat peyote and leaf fringing) *I absolutley love the look of leaf fringe so I decided to do it justice and use it just as it is titled as leaves! measures 20"*

"Donut" (spiral rope and fringing) Making the most of a beautiful donut! Measures 40".

"Peyote Gone Wild" (tubular peyote and basic stringing) This piece was inspired by my friend Jeannette Cook's wonderful and crazy designs and my friend Dave Statler's great piece of art glass. (see sources page 125). I was having a rather endless love affair with tubular peyote and just wanted to bead around anything I could get my hands on and was small enough to use in a necklace... Can you guess what the base of the bottom swirl is? A child's fun swirling straw from the supermarket! Measures 52".

"The Jester" (flat peyote and stick fringe) While teaching a class on beading a flat peyote piece following a chart, I decided to show my students how to bead without a chart in what I call "free form peyote beading" which is simply creating the design as you bead by watching the pattern evolve. Necklace measures 20" long – flat design measures 2½" x 2½".

"Feelin Blue" (tubular peyote and basic stringing) I just couldn't stop! Measures 48".

"Arbor Princess" (tubular peyote and beading around face) Grapes and grapevines circle her face and all the way around the necklace. Measures 17" long.

"Mother Nature in All Her Glory" (embroidery) Beaded leather purse inspired by my friend,
Wendy Ellsworth's beautiful leather pieces. Measures 11" high by 6" wide.

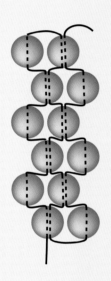

Stitch &
Technique
Glossary

Stitches
Ladder Stitch

1. Pick up (2) cubes and run them down to within 6" of thread end. Take needle and thread up through bottom of Cube 1 and down through top of Cube 2, weaving them together side by side. See Fig. 1.

2. Run needle and thread around cubes 2–3 times to secure and continue adding cubes to make a side-by-side cube line of desired width. See Fig. 2.

Fig. 1

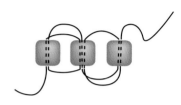

Fig. 2

Brick Stitch (decreasing)

1. Make a Ladder Stitch row of desired length. With needle and thread coming out of top of Cube 1 in base row, pick up (2) cubes and run them down to sit on top of Cube 1. Take needle and catch the second exposed thread between second and third cubes of Row 1. See Fig. 1. This will cause the (2) new cubes to sit in a slight "V" shape on top of base row.

2. To straighten V shape, take needle and thread up through bottom of Cube 1 in Row 2 and back down the second.

Note: They will slide together and the Row 2 going up will have a slight indent.

3. To continue adding cubes one at a time, the thread needs to be exiting the top of the second bead in row two. To do this, take the needle and thread down through the third bead in the base

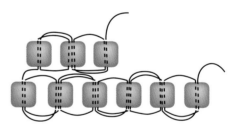

Fig. 1

row, over and up through the second bead in the base row and over and up through the new bead in the second row. Continue adding cubes one at a time. Pick up third cube in Row 2 by catching the next closest exposed thread and up through this new bead. Continue adding cubes in this manner.

Note: You will need to begin each row with (2) beads, and continue the row one bead at a time.

Peyote Stitch

1. String (6) 11/0 seed beads. Pick up (1) seed bead, skip over the Bead 6 and take needle and thread in and out through the Bead 5.

Note: The new bead should sit next to the Bead 6.

2. Continue down the row, skipping every other bead. See Figs. 1–4. Continue adding 4–6 rows of seed beads. Then begin the design, following the same technique.

Note: The first rows will be removed when you have finished the design. It is a lot easier to get a pattern started if you have something to hold on to and "waste rows" work great.

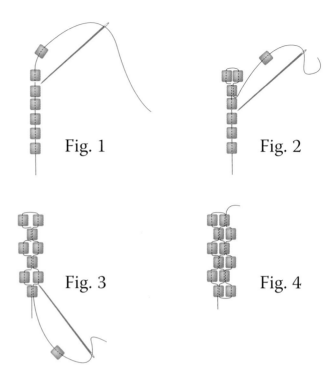

Fig. 1

Fig. 2

Fig. 3

Fig. 4

Tubular Peyote Stitch

1. Pick up odd number of seed beads and tie in circle around tubing. See Fig. 1.

Note: It is better to have the bead circle slightly loose than too tight. It takes (13) seed beads to fit comfortably around this particular tubing.

2. Take needle and thread out between Bead 1 and Bead 2, pick up (1) seed bead, skip over Bead 2 and take needle and thread through Bead 3. See Fig. 2.

3. Pick up another seed bead and skip over Bead 3, then take needle and thread through Bead 4. See Fig. 3.

4. Continue to cover tubing.

5. Weave around last row without picking up beads to tighten each end. Weave thread ends into piece and trim.

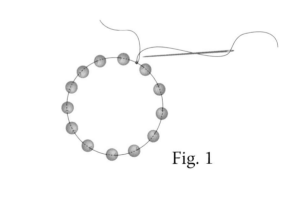

Fig. 1

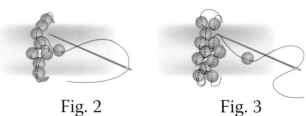

Fig. 2

Fig. 3

Spiral Rope Stitch

1. String a row of 8/0 seed beads. *Note: example uses 4 beads.* String on (4) 11/0 seed beads. Take needle and thread up from bottom of 8/0 seed bead, causing 11/0 seed beads to sit next to 8/0s. See Figs. 1–2.

2. Pick up (1) 8/0 (core bead) and (4) 11/0 seed beads and take them down to sit next to first spiral. See Fig. 3.

3. Take needle and thread up through last (3) 8/0 seed beads in core row and new 8/0 seed bead. See Figs. 4–5.

Note: This will cause second set of 11/0 seed beads to move next to core but slightly higher.

4. Continue picking up beads in same sequence, going up through last (3) 8/0 seed beads and each new 8/0 seed bead.

Notes: This will cause the continual upward spiral with 11/0 seed beads climbing the core row. Be certain to work rows in the same direction and check each set of (4) seed beads before continuing to be certain they are moving in the same direction but slightly higher than the previous row.

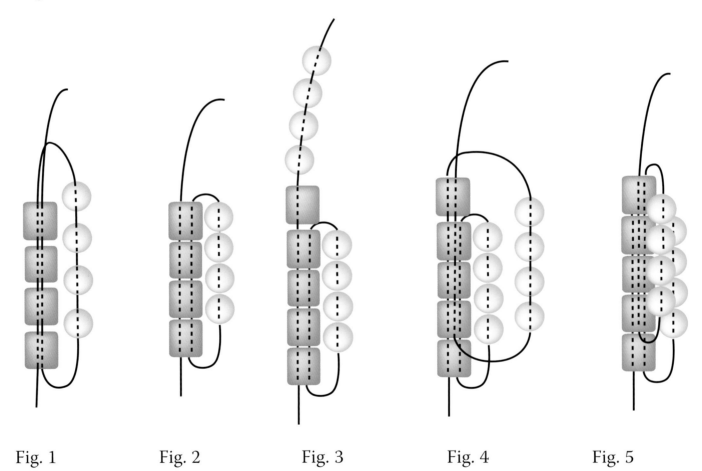

Fig. 1   Fig. 2   Fig. 3   Fig. 4   Fig. 5

Square Stitch

1. Pick up beads and slide down to waste bead see Fig 1.

2. Pick up another bead for Row 2 and take it down and around to sit next to the last bead in Row 1.

3. Attach these (2) beads to each other by taking needle and thread up through bottom of last bead in Row 1 and first bead in Row 2. They should now be sitting side by side. See Fig. 2.

4. To continue, be certain that needle and thread are going down through first bead in row 2. See Fig 3.

5. At bottom of each new row, secure it to previous row only by running needle and thread up bottom of second to last row and down through top of new row. Only secure two rows to each other as you move along bracelet.

Note: I like to work in the same direction as it is much easier. Just flip the piece after each row so you are always working from top to bottom.

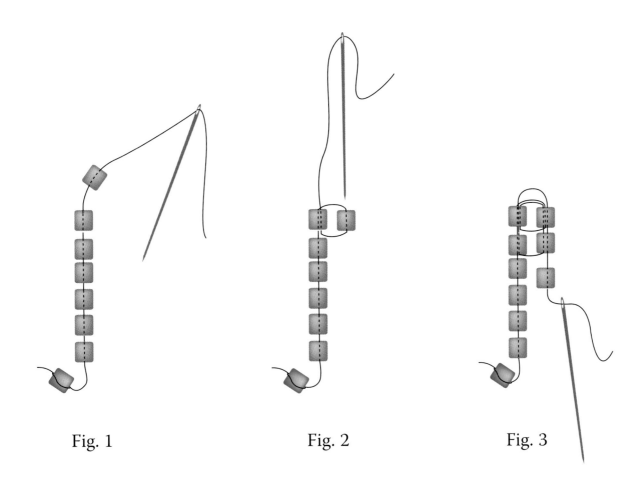

Fig. 1   Fig. 2   Fig. 3

Techniques
Coil Clasp Crimping
(for leather or silk cord)

1. Put cord into fully opened end of clasp. Using flat-nosed pliers, squeeze end coil only to fasten securely. Do this on both ends. Attach lobster claw clasp and jump ring to loop end. See Figs. 1–3.

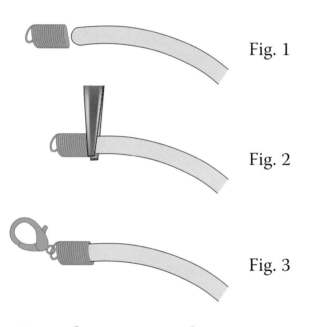

Fig. 1

Fig. 2

Fig. 3

Cord Crimping
(for leather or silk cord)

1. Place a dot of glue on one end and lay end into cord crimp. See Figs. 1–2.

2. Hold cord in crimp and carefully squeeze crimp, using flat-nosed pliers. See Fig. 3.

Fig. 1

Fig. 2

Fig. 3

Bend-cut-curl
(headpin technique)

1. Add beads onto head pin.

2. Using round-nosed pliers, bend wire at a 90° angle and cut off excess wire, leaving approximately ¼" to make a loop. See Figs. 1–2.

3. Grasp tip of wire with round-nosed pliers and curl wire forward halfway.

4. Release wire, turn it toward you so you can see what you are doing, and almost finish the loop.

5. Attach loop to earring wire, then finish the loop. See Fig. 3

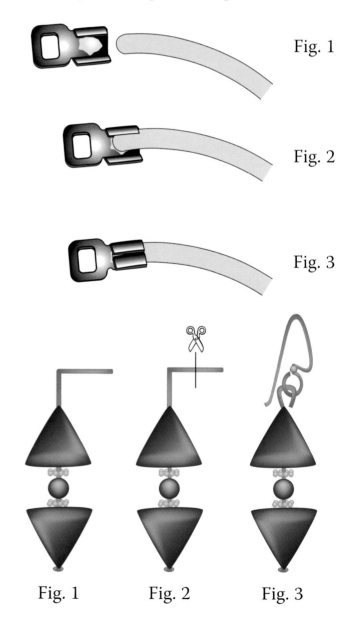

Fig. 1   Fig. 2   Fig. 3

Embellishments
Leaf Fringe

1. Pick up (7–8) 11/0 seed beads and take needle and thread around last seed bead and back out through second last seed bead in line.

2. Pick up (3) 11/0 seed beads, skip over next (3) in line and back through fourth seed bead. This will cause branch to shape a leaf. See Fig. 1.

Note: If you want more leaves per branch, begin with more seed beads on the original branch and work your way up, adding beads to form additional leaves. See Fig. 2.

Stick Fringe

1. Follow Step 1 for making Leaf Fringe; but instead of small leaf loops, just go straight back up the line adding little sticks. See Fig. 3.

Loops

1. Coming out of (1) 6/0 seed bead, pick up at least (10) 11/0 seed bead. Take needle and thread back down through same 6/0 seed bead. See Fig. 4.

Straight Small Line Embellishments

1. Pick up (1–2) 11/0 seed, a few small focal, and (1–2) 11/0 seed beads.

2. Take needle and thread around last 11/0 seed bead and back up through line. See Fig. 5.

Note: Adding (3) 11/0 seed beads at end of line will create picot. Vary order and create desired look.

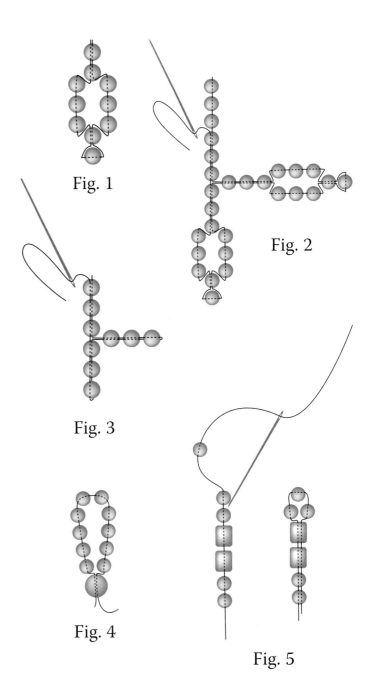

Fig. 1

Fig. 2

Fig. 3

Fig. 4

Fig. 5

The graphs shown on these pages are provided for use in creating your own designs.

Peyote Graph

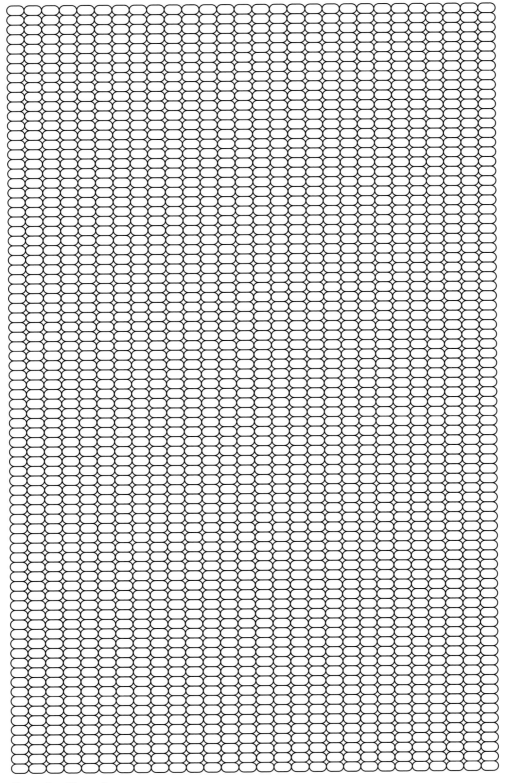

Stitch Graph

Metric Equivalency Charts

mm–millimeters cm–centimeters
inches to millimeters and centimeters

inches	mm	cm	inches	cm	inches	cm
1/8	3	0.3	9	22.9	30	76.2
1/4	6	0.6	10	25.4	31	78.7
1/2	13	1.3	12	30.5	33	83.8
5/8	16	1.6	13	33.0	34	86.4
3/4	19	1.9	14	35.6	35	88.9
7/8	22	2.2	15	38.1	36	91.4
1	25	2.5	16	40.6	37	94.0
1¼	32	3.2	17	43.2	38	96.5
1½	38	3.8	18	45.7	39	99.1
1¾	44	4.4	19	48.3	40	101.6
2	51	5.1	20	50.8	41	104.1
2½	64	6.4	21	53.3	42	106.7
3	76	7.6	22	55.9	43	109.2
3½	89	8.9	23	58.4	44	111.8
4	102	10.2	24	61.0	45	114.3
4½	114	11.4	25	63.5	46	116.8
5	127	12.7	26	66.0	47	119.4
6	152	15.2	27	68.6	48	121.9
7	178	17.8	28	71.1	49	124.5
8	203	20.3	29	73.7	50	127.0

yards to meters

yards	meters	yards	meters	yards	meters	yards	meters	yards	meters
1/8	0.11	2⅛	1.94	4⅛	3.77	6⅛	5.60	8⅛	7.43
1/4	0.23	2¼	2.06	4¼	3.89	6¼	5.72	8¼	7.54
3/8	0.34	2⅜	2.17	4⅜	4.00	6⅜	5.83	8⅜	7.66
1/2	0.46	2½	2.29	4½	4.11	6½	5.94	8½	7.77
5/8	0.57	2⅝	2.40	4⅝	4.23	6⅝	6.06	8⅝	7.89
3/4	0.69	2¾	2.51	4¾	4.34	6¾	6.17	8¾	8.00
7/8	0.80	2⅞	2.63	4⅞	4.46	6⅞	6.29	8⅞	8.12
1	0.91	3	2.74	5	4.57	7	6.40	9	8.23
1⅛	1.03	3⅛	2.86	5⅛	4.69	7⅛	6.52	9⅛	8.34
1¼	1.14	3¼	2.97	5¼	4.80	7¼	6.63	9¼	8.46
1⅜	1.26	3⅜	3.09	5⅜	4.91	7⅜	6.74	9⅜	8.57
1½	1.37	3½	3.20	5½	5.03	7½	6.86	9½	8.69
1⅝	1.49	3⅝	3.31	5⅝	5.14	7⅝	6.97	9⅝	8.80
1¾	1.60	3¾	3.43	5¾	5.26	7¾	7.09	9¾	8.92
1⅞	1.71	3⅞	3.54	5⅞	5.37	7⅞	7.20	9⅞	9.03
2	1.83	4	3.66	6	5.49	8	7.32	10	9.14

Resources

David Statler
Glass Artist

Fusion Beads
1111 NW Leary Way
P.O. Box 17137
Seattle, WA 89107
(206) 782-4535

Janice Johnson
Mrs. Magpie's
P.O. Box 3541
Allentown, PA 18106
(610) 253-8882

Jeanette Cook
www.beadyeyedwomen.com

Jeri Bellini Smith
My Father's Beads
702 State Street
Coopersburg, PA 18036
(610) 282-6939
www.myfathersbeads.com

Barb Field
Artist

Wendy Ellsworth
wendy@ellsworthstudios.com

Acknowledgments

Not that I wish to sound like I am accepting an acade-my award and want to thank everyone I have ever known; but, well, I do want to thank everyone I have known and loved as they are the reason why I am who I am and can do all the wonderful things that make me happy. Beading is my life and what a wonderful life it is! However, what gives me the most pleasure is sharing what I know with other people: beaders and future beaders alike.

I thank Jeri Bellini Smith at My Father's Beads for introducing me to beadweaving; Janice Johnson and Wendy Ellsworth for their never-ending support; the great people at Chapelle: Cindy Stoeckl, Jen Luman, and Melissa Maynard who turned my jumble of words into this great book.

But most of all, I thank my family. My son TJ was my right-hand man on this project. He reconfigured and sent e-mail attachments (I am still somewhat of a snail-mail person) to keep the momentum as fast as we need-ed it to be to complete this book. My daughter Lisa, who contributed some of her wonderful designs. My youngest daughter Cara and my husband Tom, who had the good sense to just stay out of my way as I flew through the house mumbling to myself!

About the Author

Linda has always loved beads and jewelry in general. It began when she was approximately eight years old. Her mother gave her her first set of pop beads (remember pop beads) and she spent hours rearranging all the colors.

However, she had to put her pop beads aside, go to school, and grow up. She married and had three children while working in magazine publishing on such titles as *Prevention, Organic Gardening,* and *Men's Health* magazines. In her spare time, she kept her creative juices flowing by renovating two old homes, painting, doing stained-glass work, cross-stitching, embroidery, flower arranging, and even a tiny try at quilting before returning to her real love: beading.

Linda left magazine publishing after 20 years, jumped head first into beading, and has never looked back! She will continue to share her love of beads and her newest designs with everyone and anyone who comes along with that same bead-sparkle in their eyes. "I will continue to bead as long as my eyes can see the beads and my fingers can thread a needle!" she says.

Linda teaches classes at My Father's Beads in Coopersburg, and at the Berks Bead Bazaar and the *Lapidary Journal's* Beadfest in Ft. Washington, PA.

photo by TJ Gettings

Additional Designer
Lisa Gettings

Lisa lives in Seattle where she teaches classes at Fusion Beads, makes websites, creates funky jewelry and sings jazz and classical music. Her first published project appears in Beadwork Creates Beaded Rings. Lisa is the daughter of Linda Gettings. Following in her mother's footsteps was not something Lisa intended to do, but she is now eternally grateful for the creative inspiration from Mom. You can view one of their cross-country collaborations at www.beadgeneration.com <http://www.beadgeneration.com/> .

Index